Bailing the River

Bailing the River

Poems by

Penelope Scambly Schott

Kelsay Books

Cover art: Melinda Fellini

ISBN 13- 978-1-945752-48-3

Kelsay Books
Aldrich Press
www.kelsaybooks.com

For my grandson Eli:
May you see ahead but not too far too soon

Acknowledgments

My thanks to the following journals in which some of these poems have appeared:

Adanna, Antiphon, Arroyo, Drought, Elohi Gadogi, Evening Street Review, Inflectionist Review, Miramar, Natural Bridge, Nimrod, Poeming Pigeon, Sourland Review, Switched-On Gutenberg, Tidal Basin Review, Timberline Review, U.S. 1 Worksheets, and *Wisehouse.*

And with gratitude to all my poet friends, especially the beloved women in the Cool Women Poets of New Jersey, Word Sisters, The Pearls, and the far-flung on-line Wompo workshop.

Contents

III

Perspicacity

Life gets clearer backwards.
The thing about donkeys
is they live a long time.

They know their way
to the graveyard
and back to the stable.

Donkeys perceive grief.
The donkey who carried Mary
foresaw the Crucifixion.

His yellowed teeth
ripped weeds
from the dust by the road.

You might have thought
the donkey was stalling.
He was.

I

The Woman Who Meant Well Toward the World

She asked permission before embracing
the thundercloud plum tree. The tree, birdless,
said *yes*.

Striations in the bark reminded her
of her own used flesh, how the skin loosened
and blew into ridges.

The woman worried about using up the world.
What if she ate all the potatoes or exhausted
the verbs? *caress, worship, wink*.

In the wink of her eye, all the years disappeared
or reappeared with the childhood Irish setter
or box elder beetles climbing a sunny wall.

This was her question: Was it too late
to donate her amazements
to her grown children?

And then she saw it:
how this world she cherishes is one of many,
and only this one hers:

the sofa cushions,
the charred scum of the coffee pot,
the April sky so busy with ducks.

Hero's Journey: The Female Version

I didn't need to go to war,
I bore babies instead.

I was a master of strategy:
I piled my scarce nickels

on bare edges of counters
and cooked what was cheap.

I didn't attack the citadel,
I simply outlived my mother.

I didn't star in epics,
instead I learned to be funny.

Now I am crossing the border
with my invisible flag.

In this narrow cone of sunlight
the banner unfurls.

You Know You've Become the Family Matriarch When

You have nine leaves for your table and are the fall-back
for Thanksgiving and Christmas

You can cook, serve, and clean up a family dinner for fifteen
while making it look like no work

You start a wash before driving your relatives to the airport
and remake the bed before the next set arrives for lunch

Your husband's siblings rely on you like they used to rely on
your sainted mother-in-law

All the in-laws email you, not him, about times and dates
and everything they don't eat

The simple fact that you are home means the dog will resist
letting your husband take her for a walk

You see clearly what everyone else should be doing
but mostly manage to keep your mouth shut

You smile because you have faked adulthood for so long
that only you realize you are faking

You are allowed to drink as much wine as you want
and nobody will comment

No one cares how often you need to rub lavender lotion
onto your scabby elbows

You are not allowed to allude to the truth that eventually
even you will die

You walk around on the earth gestating an emerald
that lights up the dark inside your ribs

First Astronomy Lesson

Peer up through the black bowl of night,
and hold still. Even the highest stars
vibrate and hum. From where you stand,
it's hard to tell which of the stars
are small or far. The frost-heaved dirt
under your feet shimmers like those stars
you first saw when you were young
by the lake and someone arranged stars
into dot-to-dot pictures you could almost draw
with your pointer finger so blips of stars
turned into dippers or a queen on a chair
or Orion the hunter with his sword of stars,
and you asked, Would he kill the coyotes
who sang all night on your hill under stars?
You were taken home and tucked into bed
and when you woke up, there were no stars,
no coyotes, just milky flakes sogging
at the bottom of a blue ceramic cereal bowl.

How to See

There's a special way of looking. Forget what you think you know.
Now look around you. Dots of drizzle pocking the lake. Red-tinged
finches fighting at the feeder. These blossoming horse chestnut
trees, each petal with its livid pink dot, the huge conical clusters
improbable as the great fern forests where dinosaurs might loll
about in Jurassic shade, those dinosaurs who grew up with you:
oh, yes, Tyrannosaurus Rex, yes, Triceratops, lovely Brontosaurus,
extinct, banished, and restored, each of 'em more enormous than
Daddy, and all of 'em still with us. You don't believe me? Close
your eyes.

The Details

The fervor with which I can love them
The almost invisible lizard sunning on the rock pile
The head-tilt of my white dog
The doe my dog just chased over the barbed wire fence
The doe's rotating ears as she leapt
Tidy wire twists along the fence and the softer twists
of my daughter's curls
Hairless ears of a young soldier I've never met
as he crouches behind a bombed wall
thinking of his baby brother
Not least the Jesus bug who makes this line
of tiny hummocks and indents
upon the water

Happy Birthday, Coyote

Coyote lifts her rough muzzle and smiles.
She shakes her necklace of rabbit feet.
Today is her birthday. She is seven again.
She has been seven for thousands of years.
Truth is, Coyote seldom does tell the truth.

Coyote proclaims in declarative sentences.
Likewise, she lies in declarative sentences.
Coyote lies in her stories and lies in her den.
She claims to be hatched from an egg shell,
the same blue shell that hatched the world.

Coyote claws at the bottom edge of the sky.
Sky mounts her and she bears blue children.
Coyote's babies are older than their mother.
A coyote of seven shows dubious judgment.
Her logic is impeccable but her facts are off.

It is an off fact that a rabbit's foot brings luck.
An off fact that magic rabbits sprout new feet.
Each time she turns seven, Coyote weeps.
Now she can sniff the sadness of our world.
I am seven. Coyote and I are blood sisters.

My Box of Stars

Sometimes I am the brother who flies
with one swan wing,

my crooked flight path leaving crooked
contrails.

When I was that nymph turned to wood,
my only voice

was the caw of the crow from my topmost
branch.

Crow said,

> *There was one night I loved you.*
> *Keep that night in your box of stars.*

Even a dung beetle can navigate
by the light of the Milky Way

but I cannot.
Although I am still trying

to hatch pearls
in the hot curl of my tongue.

You Can't Tell Which Way the Train Went

by looking at the railroad tracks, not even
by laying your ear to the rail, but you know
the train has departed and you weren't on it,
all those square backyards you won't peer
into, or linear towns where the postmaster
will never offer your dog a biscuit before you
cross the tracks and go home to your own
square of the universe, atoms and dust mites
invisible even as you snuggle under covers
to discover again how the dog loves to lean
against you, how the back of your husband's
neck smells like lemon or sawdust, and how
your heart beats in your hips, and you think
about trains and schedules north and south
and the old steam locomotive that chugs up
the canyon, and white paddle-wheel boats
on rivers and Cleopatra on her golden barge
as you go mucking around in large time until
it occurs to you, rather oddly, that Cleopatra
and you are closer together in history than
she was to the ancient Sphinx, and there's
nothing you can do with that strange thought
but sleep on it, and so that's what you do.

The Discovery of Pain

I watch like a movie: nothing is true:
Not my new two-piece bathing suit
not my pre-teen breast nubs

not my mother in her big straw hat
just a room with chicken wire windows
a bare room with a green filing cabinet

a coast guard officer in uniform
He opens his filing cabinet and takes out
a Libbey juice glass and an oval bottle

He pulls the stopper and fills up the glass
Drink, says the man in his uniform
Drink, says my father in plaid swim trunks

I lift my tight, red, swollen right arm
aflame from the jellyfish sting
and tip all the brandy down my throat

Outside, children still run on the beach
I hear only the biggest waves growl
A storm petrel smashes into the window

That's when I hear the bird screaming

Another Story about Language

How coyote packs sing on the dark hill
as we all keep rolling toward morning

while soldiers rumble across borders
in dusty trucks with numbers painted out.

How morning travels over the mountains
and we wake and sigh and drive to work

and feed each other cakes on holidays.
How we scrabble through days, our growls

comprehensible in many tongues and able
to be written down. How because we hoped,

we invented *despair.*

You, Grieving

After the sunlit traffic of bees,
after the chimes of the ice cream truck,
after the calling in of small children,
after the eye of the horse like a gazing-ball
set to reflect the sun-bronzed barn,

let us receive
soft talking on porches,
a breeze rising in the cottonwood leaves,
the sleepiness of regret,
the hand-smoothed sheets.

All these years of loving my dear ones
the best I know how—
patting knuckles, rubbing feet—
and yet, sometimes,
we must allow each other to be sad.

Meanwhile the Dog Just Scratches Her Ear

On a hot July day in the 1950's, three kids
mark out a square with a garden hose.
They walk the four sides.

  Their red Irish setter
  sniffs the length of the hose.

The two big girls have real shovels.
The three-year-old brother
wields a yellow-handled trowel.

The ground is stony and full of bottle caps.
The older kids keep digging.
Wet bangs stick to their foreheads.

The baby brother pats at the lawn
with the back of his trowel.
He sucks hard on the yellow handle.

  Now the dog steps onto turned dirt
  and flops down where the pool will be.

Move, screams the baby, waving his trowel.
The water of the pool will be so blue
the child is scared the dog might drown.

I want to pretend that I've swum in that pool
for sixty years. The water is clear and blue
and the baby brother is fictional.

Or not. Ghost of my lost uncle,
my mother's younger brother, boy who died
in the Pacific in the middle of World War II.

The dog I have now is a white dog.
When the sky is deep, I think she smells him.

I met him once in his tall dress whites.
I was two. Then he became my mother's grief
flooding my childhood. But how to explain

why my uncle keeps sneaking into my poems?
For all my life he's shadowed me. Please stop.
Even if you had lived, you'd be dead by now.

About Darkness

Yes, I know about darkness
My squeezed lungs under a black lake
where my young parents sit on a blanket
sipping gin-and-tonics

while I double-flip too tight
and slam
my head hard against
the bottom of the plank diving board

and how it would be so much easier
to stay down here sunk into dark mud
than to struggle breathless up
into sunshine

plus the fact that I was eleven
and never once considered mentioning
to my parents or my sister
how I had almost drowned

   Tonight the air under our top sheet
   is like spaces between the Pleiades
   like dead people's phone numbers
   inked into my address book

   Sometimes
   white-haired and wrinkled
   as if pickled for a long time
   I wake up inside that lake

Reliable Grief

Sure, sometimes it up and leaves like a sneeze
you end up not sneezing. It's gone, quite gone,
like your painful fifth-grade craving for that blue
two-wheeler with gold tassels on the handlebars.
It's gone like a drug-dealer neighbor moving out
overnight or like a packed snowball your brother
stored in the freezer. But more often, your grief
is a lover stepping out to get the morning paper:
you stand numb at the window watching him go,
even as you know he will be right back.

Show Me How to Survive Under a Heating Vent

—Tom Sleigh

I could do it.
Could worship the moment
the hot air comes on
or late afternoons when sunlight slices in.
How sometimes a wind
sings through the metal wings of the vent.
I could be a creature of skin under fur
and the fur blowing slightly
when the heat comes on.

When the heat come on
in my body between the bones
when the belly craves
without knowing what it craves
maybe it's the old rush of lilac
the smell of girlhood longing
when I first learned to sleep with a dog
me and my Irish setter
in our chaste single bed
where the dog went to bed first
and I curled around her
and she was my hot heart.
I remember the throbbing.

If I tried to explain this to my good husband
to whom I am precious
and incomprehensible
I would shiver under that heating vent
and I would be lonesome
and without fur.

April Come Round Again

How creased my fingers
How fast the clouds

Seven years ago
my mother died the day before my birthday
I stayed up all night scrubbing cupboards and closets
So little in any of them I thought I wanted

Now I'll walk in the wind in her black tapestry jacket
because I can't give it back

We Were Both Old

as we went walking this morning
in a snow globe

The dog wore white flakes
on her white fur

and I, snow stars
atop my knit purple cap

Neither of us was cold
We were both so happy

Beast

Childhood takes such a long time. Just ask any kid.
The rest goes faster and faster.

I cut off my pigtails and put on a jaunty orange cap.
Nice lid, said the tall hipster

slouching outside the tavern. I smiled into his eyes.
I was so done with waiting.

But when my baby boy squeezed out of me sporting
his scarlet skullcap of blood,

I turned into a burrowing beast. For years, my fur
tangled in spiny husks of the horse chestnut.

On the morning my baby turned fifty, my dirty paws
reverted to hands and feet.

By noon I'd dug my way out. Now I enjoy being old.
My mud-clotted snout

can almost smell the fragrant moon.

II

Even Though I've Stopped Reading *The New York Times*

When she considers the troubles of her planet,
grief is the least she can do. She does it well.

She dresses herself in brown Fels Naptha soap.
It blisters her skin. Her walls reek of bleach.

She powders her breasts with exploded cement.
Her best helmet is a scratched 10-inch frying pan.

On the odd morning she wakes up as a swan,
when her hair has turned to feathers and down,

the room smells of lakes. She sinks into silt.
There on the lake bottom, she pulls out feathers

quill by quill by quill. I used to be the swan lady.
I still own the pain. I still own the frying pan.

Woman with Tedious Dreams

I know a woman who dreams all night
of emptying dishwashers, sorting socks.
She is the daughter of *should* & *ought*.

Sure, this woman knows about evil:
stick babies with swollen bellies, birds
drowned in tar, glacial melt, more wars.

But her dreams are dull, plain, slow—
plates onto shelves, forks into drawers,
bowls in stacks, shabby socks paired.

Because creatures suffer and life
is a mess, all night long she drudges
in dreams, busy putting stuff away,

terribly busy
trying to set the world to rights.

Looking at Bread

1. Looking at a Torn-out Magazine Photo about which
   the Writer Knows Nothing at All

We are standing outside a commercial bakery
in a provincial town in Nigeria
The metal shed roof overhangs
the cement patio where women wedge
long loaves into blue plastic crates
The women will fan out
to neighborhood markets
with crates on top of their knotted head scarves
Under the bright knee-length printed tunics
flowered wrap skirts cling to their buttocks
The crowd of men in the shade of the shed roof
stand with their arms crossed
One man in an orange-striped shirt
stares without pretense
In some foreign town beyond the edge
of this torn-out magazine photo
drivers honk and a policeman in khaki shorts
with ribbons across both shoulders
stands on his raised cake stand
in the middle of the traffic circle
blowing and blowing his whistle
The morning grows warmer
I have never been to Nigeria

A slender girl in a plastic chair
lifts one hand to cover her mouth
I don't know if this is really Nigeria or not
I do know that I am no longer a girl
and no longer cover my mouth

when I want to speak
A young woman in a tight white sleeveless t-shirt
looks sideways into the camera
The woman's breasts will not always be this high

2. Something about which the Writer Knows Too Much

So here's what I know about bread and the world: most men in most places assume that some woman will feed them—it might be a mother or a grandmother or a wife or a girlfriend or a sister or an eldest daughter—and if a man isn't home he can step into a bar and a girl will bring him a jerky stick or an egg soaked in beet juice or something fried on a griddle and he will never have to think about where the food comes from because it's in front of him like the air he breathes, a blessing with which he is by right endowed, even when the bread he eats may have been carried on the heads of women, their strong necks navigating the streets like swans cutting across a lake while the men in the café sit over coffee and watch how the women's buttocks move under cloth.

In most places the men have carts or bicycles or oxen or trucks or motorcycles or scooters to carry goods from place to place, or else they have women to do it. Nobody thinks this is strange. Maybe somewhere here in America a man is pushing a supermarket shopping cart. Maybe I am a three-year-old female child with my plump little-girl thighs wedged through the front slots of that shopping cart seat. Maybe I won't ever stop screaming.

Donut Girl at Scrumpy's Cider Mill

I was his donut girl in the morning
and college professor all afternoon.
I made good donuts—whole wheat
and cider—and sold them to truckers.
One day the boss asked which house
was mine, *The little unpainted one?*
No, I said, *the big white Victorian—*
the one with the wrap-around porch.

He pulled me off the donut machine,
sent me to clean the walk-in freezer.

How torn gloves stuck to the crates,
my fingers burning red then white.
How every fifteen minutes Mr. Boss
came strolling by to watch me work.
For the rest of the morning I hefted
frozen crates of full half-gallon jugs.
I smiled. Waved. Resumed stacking.
I was never sent back to the freezer.

Protest

Don't you get tired of functional trees?
Straight rows of wind break poplars,

those corporate ornamental Bradford pears?
How they serve fastened in place?

In my next life the trees will caper.
They will fling themselves ecstatic

as a woman in prayer.
They will bend.

But never like a woman
kneeling to a dustpan.

Pornography

How barbaric the saints
strutting their grisly mutilations—

closed-lipped smiles almost smug
as they offer their truncated body parts:

two breasts quivering on a silver tray
like inverted puddings with cherry nipples.

The crows flew by in a black line
heading to feast on the neighborhood dead.

Don't think I exaggerate—
praying or *preying*, it's the same thing,

and yes, I confess it,
fervent, hazy, sexy as hell,

as if all our most tender parts
were being stung by scorpions

and we rose and raised our burning hands
and we had to cry out, *Don't stop, never stop.*

My Desperation

All my life it had accreted like a pearl
in the irritable shell of childhood.

It had no color or discernible odor
but it outweighed my whole future.

When an expedient man appeared
I offered him my desperation.

He locked me into a cozy cage
with my desperation and my babies.

Sometimes I pounded my head
against the curtained metal bars.

By the time he decided to leave us
the babies could say charming things.

My desperation went with me to work.
I guess my kids took theirs to school.

In those years we survived together
we made snow angels on the lawn.

Please, babies, my distant babies,
do you remember our lovely wings?

Confidence

For all those girls looking at houses and babies
and silverware patterns, don't rush.

Marriage is, like they say, an institution,
fearsome as high school or the state pen.

If I'd had the self-confidence I have now
maybe I could have shaped the guy up

but our knowing son says, *No,*
if you'd had the confidence you have now,

you wouldn't have married him
and I wouldn't exist.

Sometimes when my grandson sounds just
like his grandfather, I try to remember

one early morning of striped light
when my son's father and I lay in bed

pronouncing *aardvark* over and over in silly voices.
I was already pregnant.

My son is fifty-one and I'm still not sure
what an aardvark looks like,

but I think it has three *a*'s.

Sunday Service

1. First, the old Cuisinart makes an announcement

I'm forty years old and still chopping.
I've pulverized onions for a thousand curries.

She just made a mountain of slaw for dinner
She washes me well but she doesn't dry me.

I hope I don't smell moldy.
I was a Christmas gift from an ex-mother-in-law.

When the guy walked out, I stuck around.
I worried she'd trade me in for a vibrator

but there was always another guy showing up
and lordy, lordy, don't they all love to eat?

2. And now my sermon for the ladies' auxiliary

Come close and listen.
Know that men are needy but keep it to yourself.

They were born with their brains
where their vagina should be

so all they can give birth to is machines.
They are afraid they aren't bigger

than their mothers who rationed out survival.
When a man sucks your breasts, they're still yours.

Pretend to want his greedy lips.
You can be charitable. You know who made the world.

Amen. Ah, women.

Durian

I lay on the daybed among floral pillows
in thin December sun
come newly born from the far south
with its first bud of heat,
and I thought about southeast Asia
and that notorious fruit called a durian
reputed to be so stinky
people are forbidden from carrying them
on any public bus,
and I imagined the pillow by my left elbow
might actually be a durian,
its thorn-covered husk vaguely warm
in the returning sun,
and if I tucked the durian under my arm
like a prickly football
it would be as heavy as a cat
or a human newborn,
and then I thought about its ripe custard
of almonds and old gym socks,
and its scent began to condense in the air
like a fog all around me,
and I rested my cheek on the pillow of fog
in much the same way
I rest my cheek on my husband's pillow
in the first light of morning
when he caresses my belly
with a rough hand
before he tosses off the quilt
and stands naked next to our bed
and stretches and rolls back his shoulders
and shakes like a dog
so that all of his parts dangle and swing
like exotic fruits.

Rafting the River

You can stay up on the bank
like these plain brown rabbits
nibbling so silently
up in the brush.
Just like them,
um-hmm.

Or else you can raft it,
this river, these raving rapids,
this racket of water smashing against rocks,
rough frolic of wild lovers,
racheting up risk, dropping your paddle
to grab it again from the white rollick of water,
wrapping its handle with wet hands,
paddling madly through ragged foam
in the rash rushing of your own blood.
You can do that.

But for me,
it's the raucous stacking of sounds
that I like best,
the roiling tumble of syllables crashing,
the strong rivets of consonants
tacking the strung vowels into our English words—
the buzz, burrs, burn on the living tongue,
the sibilant hiss, shaped curling of wind,
glottal stop, the softest labial pop,
yes, please,
the kiss.

Warning

A bird in the house
means somebody's going to die.

It won't be the bird.

He chases the sooty chimney swift
with a butterfly net.

Her talons swipe at him.

Imagine the net as lace
a bride might draw across her face.

And the dude who married this bird?

Tell him she's really a hawk.
Say it's too late

to be talking things over.

Red Flag

One day the woman—who clearly was a woman—
decided that she wouldn't be a woman today.

Option one: she considered being her own dog.
But who'd scratch her neck and let her out?

Or maybe the beech tree at the end of the drive?
How it stood in the sky? That was a possibility.

She thought about their mailbox with its red flag—
open me, take me, feed me whatever you bring.

Been there, done that. Definitely not the mailbox.
Not the collapsing rail fence. Perhaps the puddle

left after rain? She liked how it wrinkled in wind.
But then it would dry up and vanish. No puddle

for her. She might prefer becoming a mountain.
She slipped through the window on the horizon

and rose into cloud. Later, surveying the valley
at sunset, she realized it hadn't occurred to her

—not ever—to be her husband. She saw him
without looking: busy micro-waving his tv dinner,

punctiliously punching minutes and seconds.

NASA Photo: Friday, January 31, 2014

So here's this photo of Earth taken from Mars.
Just after sunset, over the line of Martian hills.
Sort of like a star, but brighter. Imagine Venus,
our evening star. And next to Earth, a tiny dot,
our moon, the moon we love like an only child.

So imagine you are riding the rover *Curiosity*.
Sort of like a high-tech go-cart with a camera.
You're 160 million kilometers from your home
and there's no train coming. Look to the west
and slightly up. Got it? Here's the hard part.

Find the continent of North America, northwest
of the center, but south of Canada. Remember,
Canada's big. You are looking for a lighted city
but not the biggest. You will pinpoint a house
on a hill. Through the window, you spot a man.

He is busy at a desk, messing with a computer.
He is so, so far away. That's 99 million in miles.
You remember that Friday is called *Frigedaeg*
in Old English, from *Frigga*, the Norse goddess
of married love. I miss him. Where's that train?

Nasty Out There Tonight

for Eric

When branches of Douglas fir
slap against our roof,
when we wait by candlelight
for the windows to stop shivering,
when I reach for your hand
or you touch my hand
lightly, as if to make sure
we are both still here,
it's then that I feel most alone.

It's then that I curl under overpasses
or look for that doorway deep enough
to keep me dry for the night.
It's then I most want to shelter you
from ever having to consider
which copse of shrubs by the highway
could serve as the world's house.

Satisfaction

No man in my bed tonight
needing the old reassurance.
No light in the sky tonight,
only yellow street lamps
reflected in low clouds.
No skunks under the shed,
only a raccoon mama prowling
the rusty parking lot dumpster.

A happy woman can still taste
that animal joy of insistence:
sleepy peace of a two-year-old,
her lips opening and closing
around the wet knuckle
of a puckered thumb,
as she repeats, repeats
her magisterial word *NO*.

My Dog Lily

I call her *Madame Pre-rinse*
because she licks plates
and is a dog of gourmet tastes
fond of expensive balsamic
and once just once
I treated her to octopus and yes
that was a hit and I could go on
with small semi-witty remarks
about the dog or how these hills
are greening like green felt
on a billiard table but with the hills
too lumpy for billiards
and while you wait for gourmet dog
to trot back into the poem
you are beginning to daydream
about something else
like the octopus you ate in Spain
or a call you're waiting for
or why I titled this poem My Dog Lily
and then changed subjects.

Please don't feel bad if you wander
which would be just fine
because I want you to think about
whatever you think about
when you're not thinking about
something else
and for some people it's sex
which might be nice I know
I don't think about sex nearly
enough these days
I think about chores unfinished

or chores unstarted
I think about who has cancer
or how much my eyes itch
and I notice everything blooming
too early this Spring
and say *global climate change*
or *wow those magnolias*
and tomorrow the fallen petals
like a storm of pink snow
will frost the unmown lawn.

Here I could jump back to my dog
who as you know by now
is really named *Lily* not *Pre-rinse*
and discuss recipes
for keeping octopus tender
or instead I could ask you
where your mind has traveled
since you last tuned in
to my disconnected mumblings
and you may have been
someplace amazing or secret
or maybe just wishing
for a glass of decent red wine
and I could uncork it
and pour two generous glasses
so you and I could sit here
with the dog sprawled on the floor
and clink wine glasses
and say what we've been unwilling
to speak out loud
like *Come on is this really a poem*
or *I kiss my dog on her lips.*

Confession with Interpolations by the Persian Poet Rumi

He came to repair scratches on my old car.
He parked his van and called me Miss Penelope.

Judge the moth by the beauty of the candle.

Tall, late forties, curly black hair, shorts and t-shirt,
he patched, he sanded, he painted. He buffed.

This poetry: I never know what I'm going to say.

I flat out asked. He said he came from Persia.
He buffed, he polished. He buffed.

There is a candle in your heart ready to be kindled.

He hammered shut the can of automotive red.
He clicked a lighter and lit an unfiltered cigarette.

Protect yourself from your own thoughts.

The mended fender glowed red as my heart.
My beat-up car looked almost new.

The intelligent desire self-control; children want candy.

I wanted to ride away with him in his van.
I wanted to go back to smoking.

The art of knowing is knowing what to ignore.

The slow breath in. That live fire.
Call me Persian Empress of Burning Red.

Burned-Over Forest without Your Name in It

Through a forest of charcoal and no owls
on a meager hillside of old mine tailings

tramping up the rutted wagon road
passing the charred cabin

the news of fog exploring the ruins
the ruin of a piano with rusted strings

and no human voices—where last year
we walked among white twin-flowers

In the Other Kind of Time

I always want to know in my heart that there is another kind of time flowing by in parallel with the hectic conduct of man's daily life.
                              —Michio Hoshino, nature photographer

Dark green spikes of avalanche lilies
poke through snow crust in late July

Meadows of almost transparent petals
fringe the high and icy tarn

Bear grass is done and then blooming
as you move up the slope of the mountain

You can enclose its globe in your two hands
knowing the settlers called it *squaw's tit*

And the old lady who flops down onto snow—
today she is younger than words

Baigneuse

The woman in the bathtub knew she was mythic.
Rows of Impressionists lined up to paint her.
When she tilted her body toward the tall window
her pink, yellow, and blue-tinted breasts
fell plumply to one side and her nipples glinted.
Ah, say the curators with impeccable coiffeurs,
it's widely accepted that she bedded many artists.

When at age ten I was first taken to Paris,
my mother asked, did I know about mistresses?
I assured her I did. Today in my seventies
I recline in my claw-foot tub admiring my thighs
and symmetrical breasts. As the sun declines
behind the mountain peak, my faithful husband
clicks away at his computer awaiting his dinner.

Because I Wear My Flesh Like a Long Leaf

Twin to the jaguar, twin to the snake,
twin to the girl in her white muslin frock

to slink in a twining of vines,
to pause at a border of river reeds,

to share the face of jaguar,
to wear the curves of snake.

What breaks in me
is what aches to go back.

When you pursued me into the forest,
all I could say was, *I am the forest.*

This Was the Woman Who Had No Vagina

Men didn't care—
she gave excellent head.

She conceived in her tonsils
and spit out her kids.

Whenever you think you know
what matters,

Honey baby, you're so wrong.

III

Today's News

My hopeful dog is over the moon
when she finds a striped ground squirrel.

I poke the body with my shoe, gently.
The tail flops. Nope, not dead yet

but close enough that the dog
is bummed. She trots on.

Hey, we all have our problems:
my husband has crazy shit at work

and the salmon have contusions
from pounding against the dam.

I follow my dog through the woods.
She hunches to poop.

I scoop warm turds with a plastic bag
from yesterday's *Oregonian*.

Beats any news I found in the paper.
I'm grinning as I double-knot the shit.

Update

I started to write about the enormous raccoon
     crossing my side yard.
I would have described how he, or maybe she,
     stopped and stared
through a black mask over a pointy white face
     almost, I might say, as if
there were long-standing business between us.
     I was watching hard
until my computer went DING with a message
     from a friend in Paris
saying she wasn't anywhere near the shootings,
     so I turned on the radio
to hear how someone or other or several others
     were busy shooting up Paris
along with an explosion in some popular café
     near a sports stadium.
I was so glad my friend was only a fine poet,
     never a sports fan,
because she could have been the equivalent
     of a road-kill raccoon
sprawled across a charming Parisian café table,
     a table with wrought iron legs,
and then I went on to consider the non-negotiable,
     cold-blooded zeal
of such killers, and how there was nothing, or little,
     for which I would kill
a stranger. The raccoon had departed my yard
     with our bond unexplored.
I want to say I rushed to my kitchen and removed
     the cheddar from the mousetrap
but I didn't. I didn't do that. I didn't. No, I did not.

What Took the Neighbors' Poodle

When our three local coyotes
turned into Bengal tigers,
we walked our woods
with a new respect
for dusk.

We admired how black stripes
stand out against orange,
how their sleek hips
slip with a motion
like water.

Whose yellow eyes are waiting
under the black hemlocks?
Do those eyes keep pace
with your careful pace?
Don't look.

The neighbors never ask us
and nobody dares to laugh
at the big-eyed masks
we wear on the backs
of our heads.

You cannot wear enough eyes
to surprise the eyes of tigers,
and when tigers chuff
in half dark, you turn
mortal.

Whatever took the young poodle
knows the taste of hot flesh.

When at last it's my time,
then I will pray for
the tigers

to come sneaking back.
One good neck bite
can crack bone.
Crack mine.

A Smoothness

Can the earthworm love the robin
who pulls it from the ground?

Do the worm's slim corrugations
slip smoothly up through dirt?

What about a fly in a spider's web?
Does it sleep, waiting?

Back when they said I had cancer,
part of me felt ready.

A round gray rabbit hopped about
in my friend's backyard.

My friend loved her backyard rabbit.
She even named the rabbit.

A hawk came. It carried off the rabbit.
I told my friend, *Love the hawk.*

Stories

These are the stories I've told too often:
how I almost drowned in a black lake
while my parents sipped at gin and tonic
up on the shore, and how at last I decided
to come up and breathe, or how my son
almost died in a roadless village,
which isn't even my story to tell.
And then there are all those other stories
I've never told, for example the amazement
of certain orgasms and the terrible events
that followed, stories I won't ever tell
to anyone anywhere, not even if I were drunk
in some sad bar, which won't happen
because even though I seem to lack
what you might call boundaries, I don't—
they're just not the same boundaries
as your boundaries. It's all a question
of how we reveal ourselves. You'd learn
more about me if I spelled out my history
with carrot salad, how the summer maids
at my grandparents' house, each of whom
Granddaddy used to call *the schwartze*,
grated their knuckles raw to prepare
Pyrex bowls of carrot salad,
and how only in summer could I have it,
my favorite, carrot salad, though now
I plug in my food processor and grate
my carrots in no time flat. The joy.
So here I am come back from drowning,
and my son has survived into middle age,
and today in the plastic vegetable drawer
of my lousy overpriced designer refrigerator

which was here in the house when we bought it,
I have orange and yellow and purple carrots,
and now that I'm into my seventies, I care
more about carrot salad than I do
about orgasms. No, that's not true,
it's just that the orgasms I can enjoy by thinking
are reliable, long-lasting, and without grief.
Now I do my grieving for others
who are trapped inside a dark sea
and can't choose to come up and breathe,
for the summer maids my grandfather insulted,
for the hurt men I shouldn't have slept with,
for those distant dots of the stars buzzing
inaudibly as neon tavern signs
across some wide and jobless valley
where all the young have moved away.

Five Ways to Grieve: Outline for an Instruction Manual

A. Simple version
  1. Get a dog
  2. Outlive your dog

B. Long-term version
  1. Bear a child
  2. Adore the kid's fingers and the indent at the back of the neck
  3. Watch your child grow up to be unhappy

C. International version
  1. Listen to the news
  2. Listen to the news again tomorrow
  3. Etc.

D. Sacred version
  1. Beg the sky gods to prove they exist
  2. Settle for earth

E. Deathbed version
  1.

An Earlier Flood in New Orleans

We think we remember the great meals
concluding with bread pudding at Commander's Palace,
the brandy sauce,
or even the po' boy with oysters and bacon
at that little joint at three in the morning
after we'd cleaned up from the flood,
and then pecan pie—
oh, my lovelies, that pecan pie.

It's like sex remembered,
some long ago orgasm that went on and on,
and even if you left him,
and for excellent reasons,
even if you should have left him much sooner,
that one orgasm, how it went on.

But really it isn't the food or the sex,
it's the way we were young
and didn't yet believe in death,
how the night of the flood
in that basement apartment,
we were gods with our buckets and mops,
and we still believed
we could save the world and all of its treasures
by bailing the river
into the bathtub drain.

Trying to Write About a Photo of the Typhoon in the Philippines

Glaring sunlight hits this legal pad
turning the paper a butter yellow.
Our harsh south wind has finally halted.
Little tips of Douglas fir trees
barely quiver in the morning air.
Nobody is drowning in a typhoon,
nobody is tiptoeing over a makeshift bridge.
What should be on land is on land,
what should be in water is in water.
The orange Chinook salmon in Eagle Creek
have spawned in the correct home creek.

Now, three thousand miles from my son,
I can't write about typhoons or floods
or human generations of destruction,
only the new mechanical heart valve
to keep my graying child alive. Compassion,
compassion, it should be enormous
and infinite for every tree and rock
and tiny frog. When my boy was three
and someone happened to tell him
that giraffes with their long necks
lacked vocal cords, which may or not be so,
and that a giraffe couldn't call or bark
or groan or speak with any voice at all,
my boy was stricken, I tell you, stricken.
And then his plump smile snuck back.
But giraffes, he said. *Can't a giraffe fart?*

What belongs on the earth is on the earth,
what belongs in the sky is up in the sky.

Now the daytime moon is floating west
just as I flew last night from east to west
away from my son and his cut-apart ribs,
his newly revised heart, his exhausted wife,
his frightened son, their cheery brown dog
who bounces in the neighbors' yard.

Daniel Is Alive and Feeling Good

Last October, almost November,
that very last lavender rose.
I snipped its slender stem
and pushed it into blue glass
on my kitchen table. I left it.
Water got low. The rose dried.

At the end of that same October
my son had open-heart surgery
on that same heart I once felt
bump-*bump* in*side* my *womb*.
I wanted to watch the surgeon cut.
I wanted to guard my son's heart.

Late February now, almost March,
Time to throw my dry rose away.
I lift it slowly from the blue vase.
Thin white roots. Long wet roots.
How life wants to go on living.
I fetch a trowel from the shed.

West End Avenue

That's where I lived,
but it wasn't the west *end*,
it was the west *side,*
and it wasn't where anything ended,
it was where everything began,

where I still had great grandmothers
and expected to find dinosaurs
inside the curly black iron cages
of the Central Park Zoo
where if anyone had ever bought me
a balloon from the balloon man,
the string would have lifted my arm
so it pointed into the blue sky,
and if my balloon had been blue
it would have been invisible
unless there was a white cloud
like my kindergarten teacher Miss Price
told us she once entered
on the top of a mountain,

but there was no mountain
anywhere in Manhattan
unless maybe in some secret forest
in Central Park, not where skaters
skated in circles, not where toy boats
sailed on the pond, but somewhere
a train went with a smoke stack
and there were monkeys that talked English
almost perfectly, and when I told jokes
the monkeys always laughed.

I still believe in that place
and how to get there. Listen:
here comes a steam locomotive
and a conductor with wide suspenders,
and when he folds down his steps
I say *yes* and climb on board,
and when the conductor comes to my seat
to punch my ticket,
I have no mother and I have no father,
but my ticket is still good.

I Have Shoplifted Twice in My Life

The first time I was seven.
I walked one block east to Broadway
and stepped into the corner candy store.
The old man was busy selling tobacco.
Yellow cabs kept honking on Broadway.
I reached into the nearest bin and folded my hand
around a Bonomo Turkish Taffy.
I didn't really like taffy. I only wanted to be a thief.
The next time I went into the candy store
my stomach hurt.

The second time I shoplifted was about five years ago.
The check-out clerk was yakking on her cell phone.
I had bought colored sprinkles for Christmas cookies.
Plus, oh, great extravagance, a brand new cookie sheet.
The girl rang up my order without making eye contact.
She never shut off her phone.
As she bagged my stuff, I saw that in fact I had *two*
cookie sheets, stuck together. I walked on out.

The next time I shoplift
I will steal that round cloud just above the mountain
and the meadowlark singing on the warped fence post.
I'll take the high voices of school children at recess
and my grandson's unexpected dimple.
I'll stuff them away
in the hot pink kleptomaniacal shopping bag
which is my heart.

Time for a Walk

A woman sits in a green straight-backed chair
pulling on white socks. An eager white dog
stands by the chair wagging her whole body.

The woman thinks back to a long ago morning
when her old father sat for minutes on the edge
of his bedroom armchair, black dress socks

in hand. It was hard to bend in the morning.
He had no idea why his daughter's dog
should be so revved up by a pair of socks.

Today she sees her father still leaning forward
in that flowered chair, his white hair shining.
Maybe all our dead are sitting around in chairs.

Maybe if we could just tie their shoes for them,
they would accompany us on walks. And the dogs,
the old arthritic dogs, the dogs it broke our hearts

to put down, would perk up their ears and unfold
their painful back legs, and maybe even frisk a little
like they used to as we head towards the door.

Whenever I Lead a Successful Workshop

I hate it. I always hate it.
When the circle has to crack,
when the first one leaves,
then others say goodbye,
and maybe we have hugged
or at least wanted to hug,
and even as we carry away
our list of email addresses
most of us already know
the moment is lost.

Sure, first that last pause
when the molecules of trust,
like the warm intoxication
of lumpy buttermilk biscuits
lifted fresh from the pan,
still waft around us until
the instant dissipates in air
and we can only imagine
that we once tasted them,
the biscuits, the madness.

But afterwards, afterwards
there remains this tiny joy
restless as a pet mouse
riding home in my jacket pocket.
The mouse climbs up my arm
to scramble around the circle
of my collar, squeaking
The madness, the biscuits.

Big Job Being Everyone's Mother

I often carry my spiders outside
and resettle them onto a leaf.

I lift shiny slugs off the road
to the side where they were headed.

When I'm done with slug-saving
I gently uproot the garlic mustard.

I tuck clean spoons into the drawer
and slip tea cups onto their hooks.

I reset the table for supper again
and summon the world to come eat.

So much to mother around here
and centuries of work ahead of me.

But sometimes I find I am waiting
for someone to tuck me into bed.

Advice for Your New Year's Resolutions

Where a door opens and closes, stand on both sides at once.
Approach each mirror with the same kindness you'd offer a
    stranger.

If you find yourself weepy with moon fatigue, close one eye.
    If you shut your left eye, the road will be covered in snow.
    If you shut the right, snow will tumble off your left shoulder.

Always remember the holy purpose of howling.

Believe that the coyote who took your cat was starving
    Believe that the act was quick.
    Stop hunting for her collar with its dented silver bell.

Listen with complete attention to people who speak too slowly.
This year, I promise, you will have enough time.

Cruising

At least once a week
I pass my husband's old high school

On the windows of the band room
large letters still spell BAND

His unopened trombone case
grows dusty in his study at home

At least once a week
I drive by my own grave plot

Last month I got a speeding ticket
just at the cemetery gate

One of these years
I will be stopped there again

Meanwhile I don't slow down
but I always look back

Archival

This poem is not about death.
This poem is not about poetry.
This poem is not about dogs.

Wait, I'm lying.
That's what all my poems are about.
I am choosing my final dog.

She will be truer and sweeter
than any poem you know.
And she will lick my eyelids

after my exhausted children
pull them shut.

When the Rains Finally Came

The smoke jumpers unclipped their chutes
and the hotshots put down their pulaskis
and the whole line of firefighters leaped

  like goats. Like goats, they danced.

Even the rescued donkey wouldn't go home
to his barn but trotted after the crew chief.
And old Missus Coulter rocked on her porch.

She'd yelled at the sheriff: *Ashes to ashes,*
my ass. I'd rather of burnt up with my house
than to pay some damn funeral parlor.

Paying My Way Home

1

Here's why I cherish the small wind
of an August afternoon:

a cabbage moth, bane of gardeners,
flutters over the white rose.

Now the moth dips and drinks—
on powder wings, its black eye spots

wink. The motionless rotary sprinkler
reposes upon the lawn.

I can open the handkerchief drawer
where my childhood lies folded.

I can beg the trembling cottonwood
to be my long-gone father:

  Elegant. Elegant. Elihu. Elihu.
  Jangle your Roman coins.

2

I was born in a deep forest
after a sudden snow.

I spent girlhood in tight red boots.
I was born giving birth.

My son arrived like a northeaster,
my daughter like a tornado.

How the wind, year upon year
among storm-twisted ruins,

kept the three of us spinning.
I tried to dance in my red boots.

I tried to lift my babies
up-so-high above rubble.

I was born at my mother's deathbed.
After the wind hushed

nobody blamed me for the weather.
I unlaced my red boots

and walked out of the forest
into the map of the brilliant day.

3

Ago and ago, intervals lengthened
to blue shadows on snowdrift.

Clocks never struck together—
church, market, town hall.

I'd felt stuck as a child forever,
all that time waiting

for my own house and kettle,
a pile of pretty babies.

Oh, yes, babies arrived
and yes, they were so pretty.

The years. So many years.
Listen:

someone is ringing
a golden bell, and its echo

is high and long
and the same brave yellow

as the throat of a first crocus.
Today I am sucking nectar

from the bottom of its cup.

Thinking Ahead

Maybe you discovered this poem in a dry cave
and now as you examine the yellowing paper

you are puzzling over the black scratch marks.
They could be hard to decipher like Linear B.

Maybe to you the *O*'s look like small ponds
and the *T*'s like the handles of antique daggers.

What sort of language do you speak? What if
your throat and mouth don't resemble ours?

It will have been such a long time. You might
be a child of whales who staggered ashore

from an acid sea. At night do you study stars?
Once when my father was old and left the city,

he asked me, *What is that white line in the sky?*
Maybe you have traveled beyond the farthest

edge of the Milky Way galaxy and finally come
back home to tell me all about it. I'm listening.

Rounding the Horn

In a distant line like the line of an old story,
four-masted windjammers bend the Horn.
Albatross wings tilt like sails in a cold wind
that never stops. Perhaps you have dreamt
this place, gray of the far south, glacial blue
of ice cliffs, the splash as icebergs calve. If
you go there, a chip of your heart will freeze
and melt and you may weep. It's like books
tried to tell you: you think this is your planet
but it's not. You are a brief passenger here.
The carved figurehead under the bowsprit
knows more than you do. Study her eyes
as they observe the horizon.

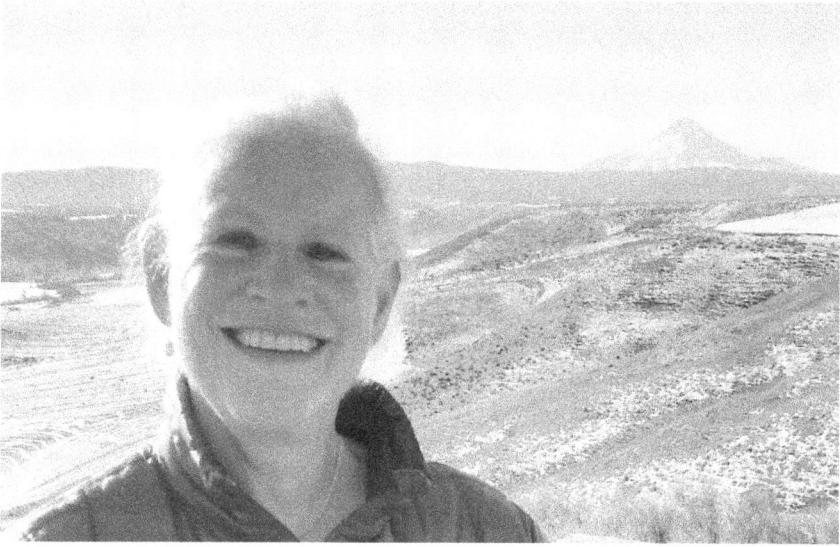

About the Author

Penelope Scambly Schott has sold cosmetics at Macy's Herald Square, made donuts in a cider mill, written texts for career guidance software, bathed people as a home health aide, posed as an artist's model, and, mostly, impersonated a literature professor. She has published a novel and several books of poetry. Her verse biography *A is for Anne: Mistress Hutchinson Disturbs the Commonwealth* received an Oregon Book Award for Poetry. Recent books include *Crow Mercies*, winner of the Sarah Lantz Memorial Award from *Calyx*; *Lillie Was a Goddess, Lillie Was a Whore*, a verse study of prostitution; *Lovesong for Dufur*, tribute to a small town in Central Oregon; and *How I Became an Historian*, poems of world and personal history. Wife, mother, grandmother, and dog person, Penelope lives in Portland and Dufur, Oregon where she teaches an annual poetry workshop.

Books Published

Novel

A Little Ignorance (1986)

Slightly Fictional Canine Memoir

Rumi and Lily: An Internet Love Story (with Jean Anaporte's
    dog, 2012)

Poetry Chapbooks

My Grandparents Were Married for Sixty-five Years (1977)
Wave Amplitude in the Mona Passage (1998)
These Are My Same Hands (2004)
Almost Learning to Live in This World (2004)
Under Taos Mountain: The Terrible Quarrel of Magpie and Tía
    (2009) (Ronald Wardall Poetry Prize)
Aretha's Hat (with Kathryn Stripling Byer, 2009)
Lovesong for Dufur (2013)
Serpent Love: A Mother-Daughter Epic (with Rebecca Kramer,
    2017)

Poetry Collections

The Perfect Mother (1994)
Baiting the Void (2005) (Orphic Prize for Poetry)
May the Generations Die in the Right Order (2007)
Six Lips (2009)
Crow Mercies (2010) (Sarah Lantz Memorial Award from *Calyx*)
How I Became an Historian (2014)

Narrative Poetry

Penelope: The Story of the Half-Scalped Woman (1999)
The Pest Maiden: A Story of Lobotomy (2004)
A is for Anne: Mistress Hutchinson Disturbs the Commonwealth
        (2007) (Stafford / Hall Oregon Book Award in Poetry)
Lillie Was a Goddess, Lillie Was a Whore (2013)

www.ingramcontent.com/pod-product-compliance
Lightning Source LLC
Chambersburg PA
CBHW071101090426
42737CB00013B/2419